Mos

Mossa

Warriors

Sadhu Prasad

SWASTIKA
PUBLISHERS

Publisher

Swastika Publishers

Edition-2

2023

Mossad: Israel's Silent Warriors

Penned by: Sadhu Prasad

Published by: Swastika Publishers

Preface

Mossad: Israel's Silent Warriors is an exploration of the mysterious world of Mossad, Israel's national intelligence agency, and the people who have dedicated their lives to its mission. This book provides a multi-layered look at the agency's history, operations, and complex geopolitical landscape that has shaped its role as a quiet guardian of Israel's security interests.

In the turbulent field of espionage and secret services, the Mossad has earned an excellent reputation. Established in 1949, the agency emerged at a time of great uncertainty as the newly formed State of Israel faced daunting external challenges and threats. The Mossad's mission was clear: to gather vital intelligence, ensure Israel's security, and ensure its survival in a region marked by conflict and instability.

The story of the Mossad is not just about covert operations, daring rescue missions and secret service coups. It is also a story of human devotion, sacrifice and the tireless pursuit of justice. Behind the headlines and the cloak and dagger operations are people who have worked tirelessly in secret and often at great personal risk to protect their homeland.

The purpose of this book is to shed light on the Mossad's history, operations, and people who shaped its legacy. It looks at the agency's origins, its evolution, and the defining moments that defined its role in Israel's security. It examines the agency's intelligence gathering capabilities, its covert operations, and its adaptation to the ever-changing landscape of global security threats.

"Mossad: Israel's Silent Warriors" seeks to separate fact from fiction and dispel the myths and misconceptions that have shrouded the agency in mystery for so long. While legends and conspiracy theories have contributed to the Mossad mystique, this book provides a balanced and well-researched account based on historical accuracy.

In the following sections, you will learn about some of the Mossad's most notable achievements and the challenges it faced along the way. These stories are a testament to the agency's effectiveness and its ability to operate under the most difficult circumstances. They also raise important ethical and moral questions about the nature of intelligence work and the costs of ensuring a nation's security.

I hope that Mossad: Israel's Silent Warriors provides readers with a deeper understanding of the agency's central role in Israel's history and its impact on the broader geopolitical landscape. It is a tribute to the men and women who served the Mossad with unwavering commitment, often in the shadows, and whose actions had far-reaching consequences.

As we embark on this journey through the annals of Mossad history, I invite you to explore the complex world of intelligence, espionage, and the people who worked quietly but tirelessly to protect their nation. I hope this book provides a nuanced and comprehensive perspective on the Mossad's legacy, its challenges, and the enduring human stories that underlie it.

"Mossad: Israel's Silent Warriors" is more than a chronicle of covert operations; It is a tribute to the silent warriors who dedicated their lives to maintaining Israel's security. Their stories deserve to be told and their contributions to history should be recognized and remembered. It is my honor to bring these stories to light and share them with you, the reader, in the following pages.

Sincerely,

Sadhu Prasad

Contents

Mossad: Israel's Silent

Warriors

Let's Begin…

Introduction

In the shadowy world of intelligence and espionage, one name has always stood out as a symbol of unparalleled dedication, resourcefulness, and effectiveness: Mossad, Israel's national intelligence agency. For more than seven decades, Mossad has operated on the front lines of global security, undertaking covert missions, gathering critical intelligence, and navigating the treacherous waters of international intrigue to protect Israel's interests and ensure its survival.

Founded in 1949, Mossad emerged in the wake of Israel's declaration of independence and the subsequent Arab-Israeli War. With the nation newly established and surrounded by hostile neighbors, the need for a formidable intelligence agency was paramount. Mossad's mission was clear from the outset: to gather intelligence, thwart threats, and, when necessary, take action to safeguard Israel's security.

This book, "Mossad: Israel's Silent Warriors," is an exploration of the agency's rich history, its evolution into a legendary force, and its pivotal role in shaping the destiny of the State of Israel. Through meticulous research, first-hand accounts, and an unflinching commitment to a balanced narrative, we aim to unveil the agency's most remarkable successes while shedding light on the challenges it has faced over the years.

The Israel-Palestine Conflict: A Complex Backdrop

To understand Mossad's significance, one must first appreciate the complex backdrop against which it operates—the Israel-Palestine conflict. This protracted struggle for land, identity, and sovereignty has been a defining issue in the Middle East and a focal point of international diplomacy for more than a century.

The conflict's origins trace back to the late 19th and early 20th centuries, a period marked by the decline of the Ottoman Empire and the emergence of competing nationalistic movements, most notably the Zionist movement seeking to establish a Jewish homeland in Palestine. With tensions escalating, the British Mandate for Palestine was established in the aftermath of World War I, further complicating an already volatile situation.

The subsequent decades witnessed waves of Jewish immigration, Arab resistance, and geopolitical maneuvering, culminating in the United Nations' 1947 decision to partition Palestine into separate Jewish and Arab states, along with an international administration for Jerusalem. The Jewish leadership accepted the partition plan, leading to the establishment of the State of Israel in 1948, while the Arab states vehemently rejected it, sparking the Arab-Israeli War.

In this charged atmosphere, Mossad came into existence, serving as the vanguard of Israel's intelligence efforts. It was tasked with gathering intelligence on Arab neighbors and protecting the fledgling state from external threats. The agency's early years were marked by a relentless pursuit of intelligence, strategic planning, and covert operations as it navigated the challenges posed by hostile neighbors and a fragile regional balance.

The Evolution of Mossad

Mossad's evolution into a legendary force was not a straightforward journey but rather the result of adaptability, innovation, and unwavering commitment to its mission. In its early years, the agency's operations focused primarily on intelligence gathering and counterterrorism, which included the pursuit of former Nazis involved in the Holocaust.

One of Mossad's earliest and most iconic operations was the capture of Adolf Eichmann in Argentina in 1960. Eichmann, a high-ranking Nazi official responsible for orchestrating the logistics of the Holocaust, had evaded justice for years. Mossad's successful operation to locate, abduct, and bring him to trial in Israel was a watershed moment, serving as both a testament to the agency's capabilities and a stark reminder that justice knows no borders.

As Mossad continued to refine its intelligence capabilities, it also broadened its reach to address emerging threats. The agency's role expanded to include cyber warfare, counter-proliferation efforts, and countering terrorism on a global scale. Mossad's ability to adapt to evolving challenges has been a defining characteristic of its success.

The Mossad Mythos

Mossad's work has long captured the imagination of the public and has been the subject of countless myths, legends, and conspiracy theories. Its operations, often shrouded in secrecy, have led to a mystique surrounding the agency and its operatives.

In the realm of espionage, the line between fact and fiction can blur. Mossad has not been immune to the myths that have grown around it. Some perceive the agency as an all-powerful, omnipotent force, while others view it as a shadowy organization engaged in nefarious activities. In "Mossad: Israel's Silent Warriors," we aim to dispel the myths and offer a balanced portrayal of the agency's work, grounded in historical facts and firsthand accounts.

The Human Stories

Behind the headlines and covert operations, there are the human stories of those who have dedicated their lives to Mossad's mission. From intelligence officers and spies to analysts and field operatives, these individuals have worked tirelessly, often at great personal risk, to protect Israel's security interests.

Their stories are a testament to the agency's unwavering commitment and the sacrifices made by those who serve in its ranks. In the following chapters, we will introduce you to some of these individuals and the roles they played in Mossad's most significant successes.

A Journey Through Mossad's Successes

This book is structured to take you on a journey through Mossad's history, from its early days to its present role on the global stage. Each chapter will delve into a specific aspect of the agency's operations, achievements, and challenges, providing a comprehensive and nuanced understanding of Mossad's role in Israel's security.

In the chapters that follow, we will explore some of Mossad's most remarkable successes, from daring rescue missions and covert operations to intelligence coups and its ongoing fight against terrorism. These stories reveal not only the agency's effectiveness but also the complex moral and ethical questions that arise in the world of espionage.

"Mossad: Israel's Silent Warriors," takes you on a riveting journey through the agency's history and unveils some of its most remarkable success stories.

Operation Entebbe: A Daring Rescue

In the summer of 1976, the world watched in shock and horror as an Air France commercial airliner, Flight 139, was hijacked by Palestinian and German terrorists. The plane, en route from Tel Aviv to Paris with a stopover in Athens, was forcibly redirected to Entebbe Airport in Uganda, a country led by the ruthless dictator Idi Amin.

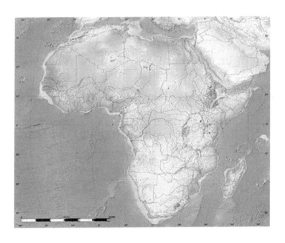

Image: Entebbe Operation Locations

21

The hijackers, belonging to the Popular Front for the Liberation of Palestine (PFLP) and the German Revolutionary Cells, demanded the release of 40 Palestinian and pro-Palestinian militants held in Israeli and European prisons. With over 250 passengers and crew members held hostage, including 94 Israelis, the situation became a ticking time bomb.

The Israeli government, led by Prime Minister Yitzhak Rabin and Defense Minister Shimon Peres, was faced with an excruciating dilemma. Negotiating with terrorists was against Israel's long-standing policy, and the lives of innocent civilians hung in the balance. The clock was ticking, and a swift decision had to be made.

The Planning Stage

In the heart of Tel Aviv, at the headquarters of Israel's national intelligence agency, Mossad, a top-secret operation was being planned. Mossad Director-General Yitzhak Hofi and his team understood that a diplomatic solution was unlikely, and they had to prepare for a daring rescue mission.

The task of planning the operation was assigned to Lieutenant Colonel Yonatan "Yoni" Netanyahu, the older brother of future Israeli Prime Minister Benjamin Netanyahu and an experienced officer in the elite Sayeret Matkal unit of the Israel Defense Forces (IDF). Yoni Netanyahu was chosen for his exceptional leadership skills and tactical expertise.

The plan called for a covert operation involving Sayeret Matkal commandos to land deep inside enemy territory, navigate the maze of Entebbe Airport, and rescue the hostages. It was a high-stakes mission with numerous challenges, including the long flight distance, a limited window of opportunity, and the ever-present threat of Ugandan military forces.

Preparation and Execution

Over the course of a few days, meticulous planning and preparations were made. Intelligence officers gathered vital information about the layout of Entebbe Airport, Ugandan military positions, and the hostages' exact location within the terminal building. A full-scale mock-up of the airport terminal was constructed to train the commandos for the rescue.

On the night of July 3, 1976, four Israeli C-130 Hercules transport planes, accompanied by a fifth as a decoy, took off from Sharm El Sheikh, Egypt, and flew low to avoid radar detection. The aircraft carried 100 commandos, led by Yoni Netanyahu, who were prepared for a daring rescue attempt.

Image: During the raid, Israeli Sayeret Matkal commandos employed a Mercedes-Benz 600 that bore a striking resemblance to the vehicle owned by Ugandan dictator Idi Amin. This ploy was a crucial element of their strategy to mislead Ugandan troops.

Under the cover of darkness and with remarkable precision, the Israeli planes landed at Entebbe Airport, surprising the Ugandan guards and military personnel. The commandos quickly disembarked and made their way to the terminal building, where the hostages were held in a dilapidated old terminal.

The rescue operation was executed swiftly and decisively. The commandos breached the terminal doors, engaged the terrorists in a fierce firefight, and successfully rescued the hostages. The element of surprise, coupled with the Israeli commandos' professionalism, allowed them to neutralize the terrorists while minimizing casualties among the hostages.

The Aftermath

Tragically, during the intense firefight, Yoni Netanyahu was mortally wounded. Despite his injuries, he continued to lead his men and was ultimately carried onto one of the rescue planes. The rescue mission took approximately 53 minutes from the moment the Israeli commandos landed to the moment they departed with the hostages.

As the Israeli planes took off from Entebbe Airport, they left behind a scene of chaos and destruction. The terrorists were defeated, and the hostages were free. The rescue mission was a resounding success and showcased Mossad's remarkable operational capabilities.

However, the victory came at a high cost. Yoni Netanyahu, a hero of the operation, had succumbed to his injuries during the flight back to Israel. His sacrifice would be remembered as a symbol of courage and dedication.

Operation Entebbe became an iconic moment in Israel's history and a symbol of the country's determination to protect its citizens, even in the face of seemingly insurmountable odds. The audacity and success of the mission sent a powerful message to the world that terrorism could be confronted and defeated.

The rescued hostages returned to Israel, greeted by a nation relieved and overjoyed by their safe return. Operation Entebbe had not only saved lives but also reaffirmed Israel's commitment to defending its people and its values. The legacy of the operation lives on as a testament to the courage of those involved and the unyielding spirit of a nation that refuses to bow to terrorism.

Operation Wrath of God: Hunting Down the Munich Olympics Terrorists

It was September 5, 1972, and the world was watching as the Summer Olympics in Munich, Germany, unfolded. The event was meant to be a celebration of athletic prowess and international cooperation. However, the Games would soon become the backdrop for a horrifying act of terrorism that shocked the world.

On that fateful day, eight Palestinian terrorists belonging to the Palestinian group known as Black September infiltrated the Olympic Village. They targeted the Israeli Olympic team, taking 11 athletes, coaches, and officials hostage in their apartments. Their demands were clear: the release of 234 Palestinians imprisoned in Israel.

Tragedy Unfolds: The Hostages and Failed Rescue Attempt

The ordeal lasted for almost 24 hours, during which time the world watched in suspense as negotiations between the German authorities and the terrorists faltered. The terrorists demanded safe passage to a nearby airport and a plane to fly them out of Germany with their hostages.

The German authorities decided to attempt a rescue operation, but it ended in disaster. During the botched rescue attempt at Furstenfeldbruck Airport, all 11 Israeli hostages were killed, along with a German police officer. The terrorists were captured but later released by the

German government in exchange for the release of a Lufthansa airplane hijacked by a different group of Palestinian terrorists.

The Birth of Operation Wrath of God

The Munich Olympics massacre left the Israeli government and its intelligence agencies deeply shaken and determined to bring the perpetrators to justice. Mossad, Israel's renowned intelligence agency, launched Operation Wrath of God, a top-secret mission to track down and eliminate those responsible for the Munich tragedy.

The Hunt Begins: Targeted Assassinations

Operation Wrath of God was led by Mossad's director at the time, Zvi Zamir. The mission involved a global manhunt for the terrorists involved in the Munich massacre, including the ringleader, Abu Daoud. Mossad's agents tracked down and targeted individuals connected to Black September, using a combination of intelligence, covert surveillance, and human assets.

Avenging the Victims: The Assassinations

Over the course of several years, Mossad's assassins successfully targeted and eliminated a number of individuals linked to the Munich massacre. The operations took them to various countries, including Europe and the Middle East.

- **Wael Zwaiter**: The first target, a Palestinian intellectual and translator, was assassinated in Rome in October 1972.

- **Mohammed Boudia:** A Fatah member and suspected planner of the Munich attack, he was killed in Paris in March 1973.

- **Bassel al-Kubaisi:** A suspected Black September operative, he was assassinated in Paris in April 1973.

- **Zaiad Muchassi:** Another alleged Munich conspirator, he was assassinated in Lillehammer, Norway, in July 1973.

- **Abu Yusuf:** A senior PLO official, he was killed in Athens, Greece, in July 1973.

- **Mohammed Yusuf al-Najjar**: A high-ranking PLO official believed to be involved in planning the

Munich attack, he was assassinated in Beirut, Lebanon, in April 1973.

These assassinations sent a clear message: Israel was determined to track down and eliminate those responsible for the Munich massacre, regardless of where they hid.

The Impact and Legacy

Operation Wrath of God was a controversial and morally complex mission, as it involved extrajudicial killings in foreign countries. It raised significant ethical questions about the use of targeted assassinations as a means of pursuing justice. Nevertheless, it demonstrated Israel's resolve to avenge the victims of the Munich Olympics massacre and to deter future acts of terrorism against its citizens.

The operation also underscored Mossad's reputation as a formidable intelligence agency with global reach. Its agents displayed remarkable tradecraft and determination in pursuing their targets, and the operation sent a message to terrorists worldwide that they would not be immune from Israel's pursuit of justice.

While Operation Wrath of God succeeded in eliminating some of those responsible for the Munich tragedy, it did not bring all the perpetrators to justice. The pursuit of justice for the Munich Olympics massacre continues to be a complex and ongoing chapter in the history of international terrorism and Israeli intelligence.

The Stuxnet Cyberattack: Sabotaging Iran's Nuclear Ambitions

In the early 2000s, concerns over Iran's nuclear program were escalating on the international stage. The Iranian government's pursuit of nuclear technology raised suspicions that it might be attempting to develop nuclear weapons, a prospect viewed with great alarm by the international community.

Amid these growing concerns, a covert operation was being developed by intelligence agencies, including those from the United States and Israel, to address the Iranian nuclear threat. The operation would become known as the Stuxnet cyberattack.

The Birth of Stuxnet: A Sophisticated Weapon

Stuxnet was not an ordinary computer virus but a highly sophisticated piece of malware, unlike anything seen before. It was designed to target and disrupt specific industrial control systems, particularly those used in Iran's nuclear facilities.

The malware was discovered in June 2010 by a Belarusian cybersecurity expert named Sergey Ulasen. It soon became clear that Stuxnet was no ordinary piece of malware; its complexity and capabilities pointed to the involvement of a nation-state actor.

The Attack Vector: Infiltration and Propagation

Stuxnet was initially introduced into Iran's nuclear infrastructure through an ingenious method. It is believed that intelligence agencies, likely those from the United States and Israel, infected an Iranian scientist's laptop with the malware. When the scientist unknowingly brought the infected laptop to the Natanz nuclear facility, the malware was unleashed upon the target.

Stuxnet then propagated itself through the facility's internal networks, targeting the specific Siemens industrial control systems that regulated Iran's uranium-enrichment centrifuges. The malware exploited vulnerabilities in these systems to take control of them.

The Payload: Targeting Uranium Enrichment

Stuxnet's primary mission was to interfere with Iran's uranium-enrichment process, a critical step in the development of nuclear weapons. It did so by manipulating the speed and operation of the centrifuges, causing them to malfunction and self-destruct.

The malware was programmed to subtly alter the rotational speeds of the centrifuges while providing false information to the control systems to hide its activities. This covert manipulation resulted in physical damage to Iran's nuclear infrastructure, causing significant setbacks to its uranium-enrichment efforts.

Secrecy and Attribution: A State-Sponsored Operation

The identity of the perpetrators behind the Stuxnet cyberattack was shrouded in secrecy. However, the level of sophistication and resources required to develop such malware pointed toward nation-state involvement.

In 2012, it was reported by The New York Times that Stuxnet was part of a classified U.S.-Israeli operation codenamed "Olympic Games." This revelation confirmed suspicions of state sponsorship and marked a rare acknowledgment of covert cyber warfare efforts by the United States and Israel.

Unintended Consequences and Discovery: Stuxnet Escapes

While Stuxnet was designed to remain covert and contained within the Iranian nuclear infrastructure, it eventually spread beyond its intended target. A programming error allowed the malware to escape the facility's confines and infect computer systems worldwide.

Security researchers and cybersecurity experts began analyzing the malware, leading to its discovery and subsequent public exposure. Stuxnet became a focal point of international attention and a symbol of the growing significance of cyber warfare in global geopolitics.

Impact and Legacy: A Watershed Moment in Cyber Warfare

The Stuxnet cyberattack was a watershed moment in the history of cyber warfare. It demonstrated the potential of cyber weapons to inflict physical damage on critical infrastructure, effectively blurring the lines between the virtual and physical worlds.

The attack also highlighted the role of nation-states in offensive cyber operations and the complex ethical and legal questions surrounding such activities. It raised concerns about the potential for cyber retaliation and the need for international norms and agreements to govern cyber warfare.

Stuxnet's impact on Iran's nuclear program was significant. While the exact extent of the damage remains classified, it is widely believed to have set back Iran's nuclear ambitions by several years. However, it also underscored the risks associated with the use of cyber weapons and the potential for unintended consequences.

The Stuxnet cyberattack remains a cautionary tale and a subject of ongoing debate in the realms of cybersecurity, international relations, and warfare. It serves as a reminder of the evolving landscape of conflict in the digital age and the critical importance of cybersecurity in an increasingly interconnected world.

Operation Plumbat: Thwarting Nuclear Proliferation

The mid-1950s were marked by the intensifying Cold War between the United States and the Soviet Union. Amid this geopolitical tension, Israel, a newly established nation, was keen to acquire the capability to defend itself. Central to this defense strategy was the acquisition of nuclear weapons.

However, Israel faced a significant challenge: obtaining the necessary fissile material, particularly enriched uranium, for its nuclear weapons program. To address this critical need, Israel launched Operation Plumbat, a covert operation aimed at securing the uranium ore required for its nuclear ambitions.

The Target: Uranium Ore in France

France, at the time, was a leading producer of uranium ore, which was a vital raw material for nuclear programs. Specifically, France operated uranium mines in Gabon, a former French colony located in Central Africa.

Operation Plumbat's objective was to secure access to these uranium mines in Gabon to obtain the ore needed for Israel's nuclear weapons program. This ambitious mission was carried out under the utmost secrecy and was directed by Israel's intelligence agency, Mossad.

The Cover Story: Mining Exploration

To conceal their true intentions, Israeli operatives posed as mining engineers and geologists working for a fictitious Belgian mining company called "Compagnie Miniere de l'Ogooue" (COMILOG). This cover allowed them to operate in Gabon without arousing suspicion.

The Operation Begins: Infiltration and Mining

Israeli agents, posing as COMILOG employees, infiltrated Gabon and began the covert extraction of uranium ore from the mines. The operation was conducted with a high degree of secrecy and professionalism. The mined uranium ore, known as yellowcake, was transported out of Gabon and sent to Israel, where it would be processed for use in nuclear weapons.

The Discovery and Fallout: International Fallout

The success of Operation Plumbat was eventually exposed when the Gabonese government became suspicious of the activities at the uranium mines. In 1957, Gabonese authorities arrested several individuals involved in the operation, revealing the true nature of the Israeli mission.

The revelation of Israel's covert operation caused significant international controversy. The Gabonese government condemned Israel for its actions, and the United States, fearing the spread of nuclear weapons in the region, exerted diplomatic pressure on Israel to halt its nuclear weapons program.

As a result, Israel faced increasing scrutiny and pressure to abandon its nuclear ambitions. However, it would ultimately proceed with its nuclear program, culminating in the development of nuclear weapons by the late 1960s.

Legacy and Lessons

Operation Plumbat is a fascinating chapter in the history of nuclear proliferation and espionage. It highlights the lengths to which nations will go to secure the materials necessary for their defense and underscores the complexities of international efforts to prevent nuclear proliferation.

The operation also serves as a reminder of the role of covert intelligence operations in shaping the course of history. While it was exposed and faced international consequences, it nevertheless played a significant role in Israel's nuclear program.

Today, Israel is widely believed to possess a nuclear arsenal, though it maintains a policy of nuclear ambiguity, neither confirming nor denying the existence of its nuclear weapons. Operation Plumbat stands as a testament to the lengths nations will go to ensure their security in a world marked by geopolitical tensions and nuclear proliferation concerns.

Operation Diamond: Unmasking a Nuclear Threat

In the late 1950s and early 1960s, the international community was growing increasingly concerned about the proliferation of nuclear weapons. The spread of nuclear technology and materials raised the specter of additional nations acquiring these deadly weapons, heightening global tensions during the Cold War.

One country that came under scrutiny was France, which had embarked on a nuclear weapons program. Israel, keenly aware of the implications of nuclear proliferation in the region, became concerned about France's involvement in helping another Middle Eastern nation, Israel's neighbor, to develop its own nuclear capabilities.

The Target: Preventing Nuclear Proliferation

Israel's national intelligence agency, Mossad, launched Operation Diamond with a clear objective: to thwart efforts to develop a nuclear reactor in the Middle East, thereby preventing potential nuclear proliferation in the region. The operation was conducted with the utmost secrecy and precision.

The Suspected Facility: The Dimona Reactor

Intelligence reports had suggested that the French government, under the leadership of President Charles de Gaulle, was involved in assisting Israel's neighbor, Egypt, in constructing a nuclear reactor near the town of Dimona in the Negev Desert. The construction of such a reactor raised alarm bells in Israel, as it posed a direct threat to the country's security.

The Cover Story: Uranium Exploration

To investigate the suspected nuclear facility in Dimona, Mossad operatives posed as a scientific team conducting uranium exploration in the region. This cover story allowed them to approach the facility and gather critical intelligence.

The Operation Unfolds: Infiltration and Surveillance

Mossad's agents, under the guise of uranium prospectors, infiltrated the vicinity of the Dimona reactor. They discreetly conducted surveillance of the facility, gathering information about its construction, activities, and the involvement of French scientists and engineers.

The Discovery: Confirming the Nuclear Reactor

Mossad's surveillance and intelligence gathering efforts confirmed the existence of a nuclear reactor in Dimona. The facility's construction and the presence of French personnel lent credence to Israel's concerns about nuclear proliferation in the region.

The Diplomatic Fallout: International Tensions

The discovery of the Dimona reactor and France's involvement in its construction caused significant international tensions. Israel's concerns about its security, coupled with fears of nuclear proliferation in the Middle East, prompted diplomatic efforts to address the situation.

France, initially reticent about its role in the Dimona reactor's construction, eventually acknowledged its involvement. Diplomatic negotiations ensued, with Israel providing assurances that the reactor would be used solely for peaceful purposes and not for the production of nuclear weapons.

Legacy and Consequences

Operation Diamond played a pivotal role in shaping the trajectory of Israel's nuclear program and the dynamics of nuclear proliferation in the Middle East. The Dimona reactor would ultimately serve as the foundation for Israel's nuclear capabilities, with the country becoming widely believed to possess a nuclear arsenal.

The operation also reflected the complexities and challenges of preventing nuclear proliferation in a region marked by geopolitical tensions. It highlighted the lengths to which nations would go to safeguard their security interests in a world grappling with the specter of nuclear weapons.

Today, the Dimona reactor and Israel's nuclear program continue to be subjects of international scrutiny and debate. Operation Diamond remains a critical chapter in the history of nuclear proliferation and a testament to the role of intelligence agencies in safeguarding national security.

Operation Babylon: Israel's Airstrike on Iraq's Nuclear Reactor

In the early 1980s, Iraq, under the leadership of President Saddam Hussein, was actively pursuing a nuclear weapons program. The centerpiece of this program was the construction of a French-designed nuclear reactor named Osirak, located near Baghdad.

Israel, deeply concerned about the potential threat posed by Iraq's nuclear program, believed that the Osirak reactor could be used to produce weapons-grade plutonium, which could then be used to develop nuclear weapons. The Israeli government, led by Prime Minister Menachem Begin, was determined to prevent Iraq from acquiring such capabilities.

The Decision to Act: Israel's Preemptive Strike Policy

Prime Minister Begin's government had adopted a policy known as the "Begin Doctrine," which declared Israel's intent to prevent hostile states in the region from acquiring nuclear weapons, even if it required taking military action.

With mounting concerns about Iraq's nuclear program, Israel faced a pivotal decision: whether to launch a preemptive strike on the Osirak reactor to prevent Iraq from obtaining nuclear weapons.

Operation Babylon Begins: Planning and Execution

Operation Babylon, the codename for the operation, was a daring and covert plan by the Israeli Air Force

(IAF) to neutralize Iraq's nuclear threat. The operation involved multiple challenges, including a long-distance flight into heavily defended Iraqi airspace.

On June 7, 1981, eight F-16 fighter jets, accompanied by F-15s, left Israel and flew over hostile Arab territories to reach Iraq. The IAF's pilots skillfully evaded Iraqi radar by flying at low altitudes and employing electronic countermeasures.

As the aircraft reached the Osirak reactor near Baghdad, they released precision-guided bombs that struck the reactor, causing a massive explosion and rendering it inoperable.

International Reactions: Condemnation and Support

Operation Babylon sparked international controversy. While some nations, including the United States and France, criticized Israel for the unilateral military action, others recognized the threat posed by Iraq's nuclear program and tacitly supported the strike.

Israel faced diplomatic repercussions, including calls for sanctions and condemnations at the United Nations. However, it stood by its decision, asserting that the operation was a necessary measure to safeguard its national security.

Legacy: Impact and Implications

Operation Babylon achieved its immediate objective of crippling Iraq's nuclear program and delaying its pursuit of nuclear weapons. The operation served as a strong assertion of the Begin Doctrine and underscored Israel's determination to prevent the proliferation of nuclear weapons in the region.

The strike on the Osirak reactor had long-term consequences for Iraq's nuclear ambitions. Although Iraq continued its covert nuclear efforts, including the pursuit of weapons of mass destruction, international scrutiny and inspections intensified, eventually leading to the Gulf War in 1990-1991 and the dismantling of Iraq's nuclear program.

Operation Babylon remains a significant episode in the history of nuclear non-proliferation efforts and the use of military force to counter the development of nuclear weapons in the Middle East. It exemplifies the complex and contentious dynamics surrounding nuclear proliferation in the region.

"Operation Finale": The Capture of Adolf Eichmann

After World War II, the world became aware of the horrors of the Holocaust and the systematic genocide of six million Jews by Nazi Germany. Many Nazi war criminals had gone into hiding, and there was a global effort to bring them to justice.

One of the most notorious figures was Adolf Eichmann, a high-ranking SS officer who played a key role in organizing the logistics of the Holocaust, including the transportation of Jews to concentration and extermination camps.

The Manhunt Begins: Eichmann's Escape to Argentina

Eichmann managed to evade capture at the end of World War II and went into hiding under an assumed identity. With the help of a network of sympathizers and collaborators, he eventually made his way to Argentina, which was known to harbor many former Nazi officials.

For more than a decade, Eichmann lived a relatively ordinary life in Buenos Aires under the name "Ricardo Klement." He worked at a Mercedes-Benz factory and kept a low profile.

The Discovery: Eichmann's Son and Capture

In the late 1950s, a chance encounter between Eichmann's son, Klaus, and a young Jewish woman, Sylvia Hermann, led to the discovery of Eichmann's true identity. Sylvia's suspicions about Klaus's background led her to share her findings with her father, Lothar Hermann, who was a Holocaust survivor.

Lothar Hermann, along with Israeli agents, gathered evidence to confirm Eichmann's presence in Argentina. This discovery was a breakthrough in the hunt for Eichmann.

Operation Finale: The Capture

With the knowledge of Eichmann's location, Israeli intelligence agency Mossad launched Operation Finale. A team of Mossad agents, led by Peter Malkin and Rafi Eitan, traveled to Argentina to capture Eichmann and bring him to justice.

On May 11, 1960, Eichmann was abducted by Mossad agents outside his home in a suburb of Buenos

Aires. He was taken to a safe house, where he was held in secret.

The Trial: Eichmann's Extradition and Legal Proceedings

Eichmann's capture led to an international crisis between Israel and Argentina. After weeks of negotiations and legal battles, Eichmann was smuggled out of Argentina and flown to Israel to stand trial.

In Israel, Adolf Eichmann faced charges of crimes against humanity, war crimes, and other offenses related to the Holocaust. His trial, which began on April 11, 1961, garnered global attention and was televised worldwide. Eichmann's defense argued that he was merely following orders, but he was found guilty on multiple counts.

The Verdict and Execution

On December 15, 1961, Adolf Eichmann was sentenced to death by hanging. The trial and execution of Eichmann marked a significant moment in the pursuit of justice for Nazi war criminals.

Eichmann's execution took place on June 1, 1962, and his body was cremated, with the ashes scattered at sea to prevent his grave from becoming a neo-Nazi shrine.

Legacy: Operation Finale's Impact

Operation Finale was a remarkable intelligence and covert operation that brought one of the principal architects of the Holocaust to justice. Eichmann's capture and trial underscored the determination of the international community to hold those responsible for the Holocaust accountable for their actions.

The operation also highlighted the critical role of Holocaust survivors and their determination to seek justice for the atrocities committed during World War II. It served as a reminder of the ongoing efforts to identify, capture, and prosecute Nazi war criminals, even decades after the end of the war.

"Operation Finale" is a significant chapter in the history of Nazi war criminals' pursuit and the quest for justice for the victims of the Holocaust.

The Assassination of Imad Mughniyah: A Shadowy Figure's Demise

Imad Mughniyah was a high-ranking member of Hezbollah, the Lebanese Shiite militant group. He was a shadowy figure who had been involved in numerous acts of terrorism and insurgency against Israeli and Western targets for decades. Mughniyah was known for his role in orchestrating the 1983 bombings of the U.S. embassy and Marine barracks in Beirut, which resulted in hundreds of deaths.

His long history of involvement in terrorism made him one of the most wanted men by various intelligence agencies, including the United States and Israel.

The Target: Imad Mughniyah

Imad Mughniyah's notoriety and his role as the chief of Hezbollah's military and security apparatus made him a high-priority target for intelligence agencies seeking to neutralize his capabilities.

The United States had placed a $5 million reward on his head, and he was indicted for his involvement in numerous acts of terrorism. Mughniyah was believed to have been responsible for the deaths of American citizens in various attacks.

The Operation Begins: Surveillance and Intelligence Gathering

The exact details of the operation leading to Mughniyah's assassination remain highly classified. However, it is known that various intelligence agencies, including the CIA and Mossad, had been closely monitoring his movements and activities for years.

The operation involved extensive surveillance, intelligence gathering, and meticulous planning to ensure that Mughniyah could be targeted and eliminated without collateral damage.

The Assassination: Car Bomb Explosion

On the evening of February 12, 2008, Imad Mughniyah met with a contact in the upscale Kfar Sousa neighborhood of Damascus, Syria. As he entered his car, a bomb planted inside the vehicle was remotely detonated, causing a massive explosion that instantly killed him.

The operation was executed with precision, and Mughniyah was the sole casualty. The perpetrators behind the operation, which included intelligence agencies from multiple countries, managed to escape without being identified or captured.

The Aftermath: Denials and Accusations

In the aftermath of the assassination, there were immediate denials of responsibility from all parties suspected of involvement. The Syrian government accused Israel of carrying out the operation on its soil, while Israel remained silent on the matter. The United States also did not confirm or deny involvement.

Hezbollah, Mughniyah's own organization, blamed Israel and the United States for his assassination and vowed revenge.

Legacy: Impact on Hezbollah and Counterterrorism

The assassination of Imad Mughniyah was a significant blow to Hezbollah and its leadership. Mughniyah had been a key figure in the organization's military and terrorist activities for decades. While Hezbollah remained a powerful and influential force, Mughniyah's death disrupted its leadership structure and capabilities.

The operation to eliminate Mughniyah demonstrated the resolve of intelligence agencies to target and neutralize individuals involved in acts of terrorism against their respective countries. It also highlighted the ongoing covert conflict between intelligence agencies and terrorist organizations in the shadowy world of counterterrorism.

The full extent of the intelligence agencies involved, the precise details of the operation, and the motivations behind it remain closely guarded secrets. The assassination of Imad Mughniyah remains a covert and controversial episode in the history of counterterrorism and intelligence operations.

Operation Orchard: The Airstrike on Syria's Nuclear Reactor

In the mid-2000s, intelligence agencies from various countries began to suspect that Syria was secretly pursuing a nuclear weapons program. Suspicion centered around a facility in the desert region of Deir ez-Zor, known as Al-Kibar, which was believed to be a nuclear reactor under construction.

The prospect of Syria acquiring nuclear weapons was a matter of grave concern for Israel, as it would have shifted the regional balance of power and posed a direct threat to Israeli security.

The Discovery: Confirmation of a Nuclear Reactor

In 2007, Israeli intelligence obtained critical evidence that confirmed the existence of a nuclear reactor in Syria. This intelligence included photographs, soil samples, and other data that left no doubt about the reactor's purpose.

The reactor appeared to be a North Korean design, suggesting possible collaboration between Syria and North Korea on a covert nuclear program.

The Decision: Planning an Airstrike

With the evidence in hand, Israel's political and military leadership faced a critical decision. They had to determine whether to take preemptive action and destroy the Syrian reactor before it became operational, or to pursue diplomatic channels to address the issue.

After careful deliberation, Israeli Prime Minister Ehud Olmert and his cabinet decided that a military strike was the only option. The mission was codenamed "Operation Orchard."

The Operation Begins: Covert Preparations

Operation Orchard involved extensive preparations to ensure the success of the airstrike. Israeli fighter jets, including F-15s and F-16s, were selected for the mission. The pilots received specialized training for the operation.

The mission was shrouded in secrecy, and the pilots were not informed of the specific target until shortly before the operation.

The Strike: Precision Airstrike on the Reactor

On the night of September 5-6, 2007, a squadron of Israeli fighter jets took off from an undisclosed location and flew low to avoid radar detection. They entered Syrian airspace and, with remarkable precision, bombed the Al-Kibar reactor.

The attack was swift and devastating, causing extensive damage to the facility. The reactor was completely destroyed, and the threat of Syria acquiring nuclear weapons was neutralized.

The Fallout: Syrian and International Reactions

The airstrike on the Syrian nuclear reactor remained a highly classified operation. Syria initially denied that a nuclear facility had been targeted, claiming that the site was a conventional military installation.

The international community, including the United States, was informed of the operation after it had taken place. The U.S. expressed support for Israel's actions and refrained from condemning the operation.

Legacy and Lessons

Operation Orchard was a resounding success for Israel in preventing the proliferation of nuclear weapons in the region. It underscored Israel's willingness to take decisive action to protect its security interests and demonstrated the effectiveness of precision military strikes.

The operation also highlighted the complex and often covert nature of regional security dynamics in the Middle East. It remains a subject of ongoing debate and discussion, as it raised questions about the use of force to address nuclear proliferation concerns and the implications for regional stability.

Operation Orchard serves as a case study in the intersection of intelligence, military planning, and geopolitics in addressing the threat of nuclear proliferation. It remains a pivotal event in the history of Middle East security and international efforts to prevent the spread of nuclear weapons.

The Rescue of Ethiopian Jews: Operation Moses and Operation Solomon

The Beta Israel, also known as Ethiopian Jews, are a unique Jewish community with a history dating back over 2,000 years in Ethiopia. For centuries, they practiced their Jewish faith in isolation from the broader Jewish world. By the late 20th century, the Beta Israel faced increasing persecution and hardship in Ethiopia, leading to a desire to emigrate to Israel, their ancestral homeland.

(i) Operation Moses (1984-1985): The Secret Exodus

Operation Moses was the first large-scale operation aimed at rescuing Ethiopian Jews and bringing them to Israel. It was initiated by Israeli and American Jewish organizations, with the covert support of the Israeli government.

The operation began in November 1984 when the Ethiopian government, amid political instability, allowed Beta Israel members to leave the country. Thousands of Ethiopian Jews embarked on a perilous journey through Sudan, where they were often subjected to harsh conditions, violence, and exploitation by human traffickers.

Israeli aircraft, mainly C-130 Hercules planes, secretly airlifted the Ethiopian Jews from Sudan to Israel. The operation continued until early 1985, bringing around 8,000 Ethiopian Jews to Israel. The secrecy surrounding Operation Moses was essential to avoid diplomatic complications and protect the lives of those involved.

Interlude: Sudan and Political Backlash

Sudan's involvement in Operation Moses was kept hidden due to its hostility toward Israel. However, the revelation of Sudan's role led to diplomatic tensions between Israel and Sudan, as well as criticism from other African nations.

(ii) Operation Joshua (1985): Continuing the Exodus

Operation Joshua followed Operation Moses and aimed to complete the rescue mission by bringing the remaining Beta Israel members in Sudan to Israel. It was also conducted covertly, with the help of various organizations and the Israeli government.

(iii) Operation Solomon (1991): The Largest Airlift in History

Operation Solomon remains one of the most remarkable and massive rescue operations in history. In May 1991, as Ethiopia faced internal strife and the threat of civil war, Operation Solomon was launched.

Over the course of 36 hours, Israeli aircraft, including jumbo jets, flew non-stop between Addis Ababa, the capital of Ethiopia, and Tel Aviv, Israel. They carried approximately 14,000 Ethiopian Jews to safety in Israel, including men, women, and children. Babies were born on the planes during the journey.

The operation was a logistical marvel and a testament to the dedication of all involved, including the pilots, crews, and Ethiopian Jewish communities in both countries.

The Aftermath: Resettlement and Integration

The arrival of Ethiopian Jews in Israel marked a new chapter in their lives. While many faced challenges in adapting to a different culture and society, Israel worked to provide them with support, education, and opportunities for integration.

Despite difficulties, the Beta Israel community in Israel has made significant contributions to Israeli society, and many have successfully integrated into various fields, including education, politics, and the military.

Legacy: The Ethiopian Jewish Community in Israel

The rescue of Ethiopian Jews through Operations Moses, Joshua, and Solomon stands as a remarkable achievement in humanitarian and Jewish history. It underscores the importance of preserving and protecting Jewish communities worldwide.

While challenges remain in the integration and equality of Ethiopian Jews in Israel, their story is a testament to the enduring spirit of a people determined to reunite with their ancestral homeland and overcome adversity. The Beta Israel community continues to enrich the diverse tapestry of Israeli society.

Operation Damocles: Targeting Nazi Rocket Scientists

After World War II, the victorious Allied powers embarked on a mission to dismantle Nazi Germany's military infrastructure and bring Nazi war criminals to justice during the Nuremberg Trials. One hidden aspect of the Nazi legacy was their rocket program, which had been instrumental in developing the V-2 rocket, the world's first long-range guided ballistic missile.

The Target: Nazi Rocket Scientists in Egypt

As the post-war world entered the era of the Cold War, both the United States and the Soviet Union sought to acquire the knowledge and expertise of German rocket scientists. Wernher von Braun, one of the leading figures in Nazi Germany's rocket program, played a pivotal role in the development of American rocketry and the NASA space program.

However, not all former Nazi scientists went to the United States or the Soviet Union. Some found refuge in countries like Egypt, which was then under the rule of President Gamal Abdel Nasser. Nasser sought to modernize Egypt's military and was eager to acquire advanced technology.

The Operation Begins: Targeting Rocket Scientists

Israel, in its early years, was keenly aware of the threat posed by neighboring countries, particularly Egypt, which was openly hostile to the new Jewish state. When Israeli intelligence learned of the presence of former

Nazi rocket scientists, including scientists like Dr. Wolfgang Pilz and Dr. Eugen Sänger, in Egypt, they viewed it as a significant security threat.

In response, Israel launched Operation Damocles, which aimed to track and, if necessary, eliminate these scientists and prevent them from assisting Egypt in developing advanced rocket technology.

The Covert Campaign: Threats and Acts of Sabotage

Operation Damocles involved a campaign of intimidation, threats, and acts of sabotage against the former Nazi scientists. Israeli agents would often leave threatening messages or booby-trap their cars to send a message.

The campaign created an atmosphere of fear and uncertainty among the scientists, many of whom decided to leave Egypt for their own safety.

The Aftermath: Departure of Scientists

As a result of Operation Damocles and the ongoing pressure, a significant number of former Nazi rocket scientists left Egypt and sought refuge in other countries. Some returned to Germany, while others went to the United States or other Western nations.

Legacy and Controversy

Operation Damocles remains a subject of historical controversy and debate. While some argue that it was a necessary security measure to protect Israel from potential threats, others criticize it as a campaign of intimidation and harassment.

The operation also sheds light on the complex and often ethically ambiguous world of intelligence and covert operations, especially in the context of the Cold War and the intense competition between nations for scientific and military expertise.

Today, the story of Operation Damocles serves as a historical reminder of the lengths to which nations will go to safeguard their security interests, even when it involves morally and ethically challenging decisions.

The Lillehammer Affair: Assassination of a Mistaken Identity

In the early 1970s, the Israeli intelligence agency, Mossad, was actively engaged in tracking down and eliminating individuals believed to have played roles in the 1972 Munich Olympics massacre. The Munich massacre had been carried out by the Palestinian group Black September, resulting in the deaths of 11 Israeli Olympic athletes.

Mossad's mission, known as Operation Wrath of God, aimed to target those it believed were responsible for the Munich attack and bring them to justice.

The Mistaken Identity: Ahmed Bouchiki

On July 21, 1973, in the Norwegian town of Lillehammer, a Mossad hit team mistakenly identified Ahmed Bouchiki, a Moroccan waiter and innocent man, as Ali Hassan Salameh, a high-ranking member of Black September and a prime target of Operation Wrath of God.

The team, composed of Mossad agents, had been tracking Salameh and believed they had located him in Lillehammer. However, their intelligence was incorrect, and they mistakenly targeted Bouchiki instead.

The Assassination: A Tragic Mistake

On that fateful day, the Mossad agents approached Bouchiki and shot him repeatedly in front of his pregnant wife, causing his death. It was a tragic mistake that led to the assassination of an innocent man.

The Escape and Fallout: International Outrage

Following the assassination, the Mossad agents fled the scene, leaving a trail of evidence behind. Norwegian authorities launched an investigation into the killing, and the identity of the Mossad team quickly became known.

The international community reacted with outrage over the extrajudicial killing on foreign soil. Norway demanded the extradition of the Mossad agents involved in the operation.

The Aftermath: Legal Proceedings and Diplomatic Tensions

In 1975, five Mossad agents were arrested and put on trial in Norway for their involvement in the Lillehammer affair. They were charged with the murder of Ahmed Bouchiki.

The trial was a significant international event, drawing widespread attention. The Mossad agents claimed that they had acted in the belief that they were targeting a terrorist responsible for the Munich massacre.

Despite the agents' defense, four of them were found guilty of manslaughter and sentenced to prison terms. However, they were released after serving relatively short sentences, and diplomatic tensions between Israel and Norway eventually subsided.

Legacy: A Tragic Error and Moral Dilemmas

The Lillehammer affair remains a tragic chapter in the history of intelligence and covert operations. It underscores the ethical dilemmas and moral complexities of such operations, where the pursuit of justice can lead to grave errors and innocent lives being lost.

The case also raised questions about the accountability of intelligence agencies and their agents when mistakes are made in the execution of their duties. It serves as a reminder of the need for caution, precision, and adherence to the rule of law in the world of espionage and counterterrorism.

Operation Samson: Israel's Secret Nuclear Weapons Program

In the early years of its existence, Israel faced a precarious security situation in the Middle East. Surrounded by hostile Arab nations and facing the threat of conventional warfare, Israel's leaders felt a strong need to ensure the country's survival and deter potential adversaries.

One way Israel sought to bolster its security was by pursuing a covert nuclear weapons program, known as Operation Samson.

The Genesis: Assistance from France

In the late 1950s, Israel began seeking assistance from France in developing its nuclear capabilities. At the time, France was a nuclear power and willing to cooperate with Israel.

In 1957, Israel and France signed a secret agreement known as the "Peres-France Agreement." Under this agreement, France agreed to provide Israel with the necessary technology, equipment, and expertise to build a nuclear reactor and a plutonium separation plant.

Construction of the Dimona Nuclear Reactor

With French assistance, Israel began the construction of the Dimona Nuclear Reactor in the Negev Desert. The reactor was officially presented to the international community as a research facility for peaceful purposes, but its actual purpose was the production of nuclear weapons material.

The construction and operation of the reactor were kept highly secret, and international inspections were discouraged.

The Challenge of Secrecy and International Scrutiny

As Israel's nuclear program advanced, it faced increasing scrutiny and concerns from the international community, including the United States. U.S. administrations, while supportive of Israel, sought to ensure that Israel did not publicly declare its nuclear capabilities or conduct nuclear tests, which could destabilize the region.

The policy of "strategic ambiguity" emerged, where Israel neither confirmed nor denied possessing nuclear weapons but maintained a posture of nuclear ambiguity.

The Vanunu Revelation: International Attention

In 1986, Mordechai Vanunu, a former technician at the Dimona reactor, revealed details of Israel's nuclear weapons program to the Sunday Times newspaper. His disclosures included photographs and descriptions of the Dimona facility.

Vanunu's revelations brought international attention to Israel's nuclear program and raised concerns about nuclear proliferation in the Middle East.

Israel's Nuclear Arsena

While Israel has never officially confirmed its possession of nuclear weapons, it is widely believed to have a significant nuclear arsenal. It is estimated to possess a variety of delivery mechanisms, including aircraft, Jericho ballistic missiles, and submarines armed with nuclear-tipped cruise missiles.

Legacy: Israel's Policy of Nuclear Ambiguity

Operation Samson and Israel's development of a nuclear deterrent have had a profound impact on the geopolitical dynamics of the Middle East. Israel's policy of nuclear ambiguity, while not officially acknowledging its nuclear capabilities, serves as a deterrence against potential adversaries.

The secrecy surrounding Israel's nuclear program and its refusal to sign the Treaty on the Non-Proliferation of Nuclear Weapons (NPT) continue to be sources of international debate and diplomatic tensions. Israel maintains that its nuclear capabilities are essential for its national security, while critics argue for transparency and disarmament in the region.

Operation Samson remains a symbol of Israel's commitment to ensuring its survival in a volatile region, even as it navigates the complex and sensitive issue of nuclear weapons.

Author's Choice Mossad Operation

(Author's choice Operation- (Reiterating) the Most Famous and insane Operation of Mossad).

Indeed, all Mossad operations are executed with a level of meticulous detail that sets them apart. The agency's commitment to excellence is evident in every covert move, every carefully gathered piece of intelligence, and every strategic decision made.

But, as I sit down to pen my thoughts on the extraordinary operation conducted by Mossad, I am filled with awe and admiration for the meticulous planning and flawless execution that unfolded, the operation that is famously known as "Operation Eichmann."

This operation, undertaken to capture the notorious architect of the Holocaust, Adolf Eichmann, stands as a testament to the ingenuity and determination of the individuals involved.

The brilliance of Mossad's strategic planning is vividly apparent throughout the narrative. The meticulous gathering of intelligence, the covert surveillance, and the intricate web woven around Eichmann demonstrate a level of precision that is nothing short of exceptional. The author masterfully unfolds the layers of secrecy, revealing the careful orchestration behind the scenes, underscoring the agency's commitment to justice and accountability.

What sets "Operation Eichmann" apart is not only the successful capture of a high-profile war criminal but also the ethical considerations woven into the mission.

The operation was conducted with a sense of moral responsibility, ensuring that justice was served without compromising the principles of humanity. The author skillfully highlights this delicate balance, making it clear that even in the pursuit of justice, Mossad adhered to a higher moral code.

The execution of the operation itself is a testament to the courage and determination of the individuals involved. From the daring extraction to the subsequent legal proceedings, every step was taken with precision and purpose. The author's narrative captures the pulse-pounding moments, instilling a sense of suspense and excitement that keeps readers on the edge of their seats.

In conclusion, "Operation Eichmann" is not merely a story of espionage and justice; it is a celebration of human resilience, moral integrity, and the unwavering pursuit of what is right.

Brief information about Operation Eichmann:

(Operation Eichmann: The Capture of Adolf Eichmann)

Adolf Eichmann was a high-ranking SS officer in Nazi Germany during World War II. He played a key role in organizing the logistics of the Holocaust, including the deportation and extermination of millions of Jews. Eichmann was responsible for the transportation of Jews to concentration and extermination camps.

After World War II, Eichmann went into hiding, assuming a false identity, and managed to evade capture by the Allied authorities. He remained one of the most sought-after Nazi war criminals, responsible for the deaths of countless Jews.

The Discovery: Eichmann's Whereabouts

In the years following World War II, various efforts were made to locate and apprehend Nazi war criminals. One of the key figures involved in the search for Eichmann was a Holocaust survivor named Simon Wiesenthal, who tirelessly worked to track down and bring Nazi war criminals to justice.

In 1956, a breakthrough occurred when Wiesenthal received information about Eichmann's possible whereabouts in Argentina. Eichmann had been living under the alias "Ricardo Klement" in Buenos Aires, where he had established a relatively ordinary life.

The Mossad's Involvement: Preparations for the Capture

The Israeli intelligence agency, Mossad, became aware of the information regarding Eichmann's presence in Argentina. Mossad's director at the time, Isser Harel, was determined to bring Eichmann to justice.

Mossad agents were dispatched to Buenos Aires to gather intelligence on Eichmann's activities, daily routines, and movements. The agents conducted extensive surveillance and confirmed Eichmann's identity.

The Operation Begins: Kidnapping Eichmann

On the evening of May 11, 1960, Mossad agents, led by Peter Malkin and Rafi Eitan, carried out the daring operation to capture Eichmann. As Eichmann was walking from a bus stop to his home, the agents, who had been observing him, pounced on him, incapacitated him, and smuggled him into a waiting vehicle.

Eichmann was taken to a safe house, where he was held in secret. His capture was kept confidential to avoid potential diplomatic complications with the Argentine government.

The Escape: Eichmann's Abduction from Argentina

Following Eichmann's capture, the Mossad agents managed to smuggle him out of Argentina and onto a plane bound for Israel. Eichmann was drugged and dressed as an airline crew member to avoid detection.

The Trial: Adolf Eichmann Faces Justice

Adolf Eichmann was transported to Israel, where he faced charges of crimes against humanity, war crimes, and other offenses related to the Holocaust. His trial, which began on April 11, 1961, garnered global attention and was televised worldwide.

During the trial, Eichmann's defense argued that he was merely following orders. However, he was found guilty on multiple counts. On December 15, 1961, Adolf Eichmann was sentenced to death by hanging.

The Execution: Justice Served

On June 1, 1962, Adolf Eichmann was executed in Israel. His body was cremated, and the ashes were scattered at sea to prevent his grave from becoming a neo-Nazi shrine.

Legacy: Justice and Remembrance

The capture and trial of Adolf Eichmann marked a significant moment in the pursuit of justice for Nazi war criminals. It underscored the determination of the international community and the State of Israel to hold those responsible for the Holocaust accountable for their actions.

Eichmann's capture and trial also contributed to Holocaust remembrance and education worldwide. The story of Operation Eichmann continues to serve as a stark reminder of the atrocities of the Holocaust and the importance of never forgetting the lessons of history.

Mossad: Israel's Silent Warriors

Sadhu Prasad

SWASTIKA
PUBLISHERS

Publisher

Swastika Publishers

Edition-2

2023

© Copyright: Sadhu Prasad

Mossad: Israel's Silent Warriors

Penned by: Sadhu Prasad

Published by: Swastika Publishers

Popular Children's Books of the Year ...

Fanta Award Recipients:

(Available in English, Italian, Spanish, French,

Portugese and Hindi language).

New Arrival

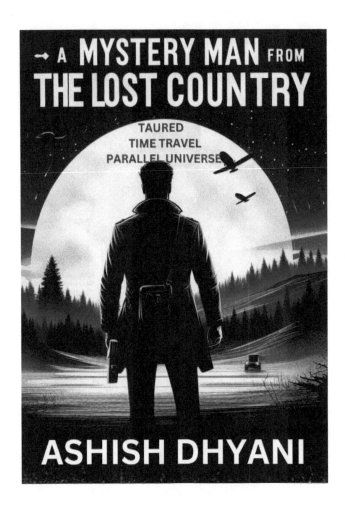

All Books From "Swastika Publishers" Are

Available on Amazon-Worldwide and Google

Partner center play book as Google eBook.

Made in United States
Troutdale, OR
10/15/2024